THE FELONY

(a story of social injustice since thousand years)

Sunil Kumar Sahoo

First Published in August 2021
ISBN: 978-93-5472-150-2

BLUEROSE PUBLISHERS
www.bluerosepublishers.com
info@bluerosepublishers.com
+91 8882 898 898
Distributed by: BlueRose, Amazon, Flipkart, Shopclues

Wordsbrew

Dedication

To My Mother

Who taught me the real meaning of Life

Who stood by me & hold my hand when I ------------

(Love you Bou)

Preface

Although it had been known since 1981 that Hansen's disease is easily curable with MDT and it is the least infectious of all diseases, to date in the 21st century, Hansen's disease is still viewed as a metaphor and treated like a myth. This problem is not unique to one country, one state or continent Rather; it is a global problem.

A strong and united stance should be taken by the general public, the person experienced with Hansen's disease and social activists to protect the rights of individual experienced from Hansen's disease. It is the perfect time, the person experienced with Hansen's disease who are represented in various forums to take a strong stance about the ground root problem. There is a famous saying that even the mother does not feed a child until it cries.

Our efforts have reached milestone and have achieved a landmark in terms of social justice in the arenas of gender, religion, race, and disability. Our attention has been drawn away from the oldest human rights issue of the world: Hansen's disease and the rights of its victims. In the present day they are still battling for dignity.

Despite the fact that human ears can hear a voice from 20 to 20000Hz, it is likely that the voice of oldest human rights issue of the world was not heard because they are still fighting for their basic needs such as food& shelter. It is well said that, an impoverished voice can't speak about revolution, the old adage goes.

Due to a friend, philosopher and guide Dr. Alice Cruz, United Nations Special Rapporteur, now finally, I am able to publish my poetry collection in 2021.

This poetry is a wakeup call with the aim of motivating millions of people across the globe, to join hands and become the voice of the millions who to date are living an undignified life.

Injustice is a concept that should not be in the dictionary, a lesson Hansen's disease teaches.

Sunil Kumar Sahoo

Acknowledgement

There are people in this world some of them are so wonderful and friendly who motivates you and act as a mentor in your life. I would like to express the deepest gratitude to United Nations Special Rapporteur Dr. Alice Cruz who is a friend, philosopher and a guide for her encouragement & support. A belief was developed in our mind that we can make a difference and that every voice matters.

Furthermore, I am grateful for the encouragement and support I have received from the Global Group.

As a final thank you to my wife, my soul mate, Sonali for her unwavering support each and every step of the way, my deepest gratitude for your encouragement during the toughest times.

About the Book

A profound collection of poems inspired by real life sufferings of person experienced with Hansen's disease, who were institutionalized, separated, castrated, and confined to a miserable life, (although different treatments were available for Hansen's disease since ages). Millions of people have died of various diseases in the past due to Black Death(Plague), Small Pox, SARS, Influenza, Diarrhea etc. People were able to lead a dignified life once they were cured of it. In addition, neither the people suffering from any kind of disease were institutionalized or forced to separate. However, Person experienced with Hansen's disease was subjected to inhumane torture for thousands of years just because of an archaic belief. Different texts reveal, however, that Hansen's disease could be treated even in 600 B.C.

At the end of 19th century, Hansen's disease was criminalized in the name of "An act to prevent the spread" that lasted almost a century later. Under the law, anyone suspected of having Hansen's disease was arrested and exiled regardless of their age, race, or gender.

The poem collection, tells the story of a kid exiled from his family and left to live alone on an island, social, legal, &religious discrimination against Hansen's disease, an exiled lover is separated from his beloved and exiled to an island & the ugly truth of the society.

The truth is life is not so beautiful as it appears in literature, similarly, no literature, no movie based on real-life incidence can show you the true pain & suffering that a person who has experienced atrocities has gone through. The only way to feel the atrocities is to go through them yourself.

A civil death occurs when a person loses all of or almost all of their civil rights either as a result of a conviction for a felony or as a result of legislation for a felony or as a result of legislation enacted by the Government of a country.

One of the world's most famous saying is "When the world is silent, even one voice can make a difference." To make the world aware of the truth, we must be that voice and show the true face of Hansen's disease which is mistakenly labeled just as a disease like any other not as a social disability.

My heart broke when found out that few persons experienced from Hansen's disease also do not recognize the enormity of the problem and only consider the medical aspects and not the social one. I believe these are the reasons for publishing the poetry, I hope it will be able to create ripples in people's mind and the collective voice will make a difference.

Our efforts have reached milestone and have achieved a landmark in terms of social justice in the arenas of gender, religion, race, and disability. Our attention has been drawn away from the oldest human rights issue of the world: Hansen's disease and the rights of its victims. In the present day they are still battling for dignity.

Despite the fact that human ears can hear a voice from 20 to 20000Hz, it is likely that the voice of oldest human rights issue of the world was not heard because they are still fighting for their basic needs such as food& shelter. It is well said that, an impoverished voice can't speak about revolution, the old adage goes.

Throughout the ages, people experienced from Hansen's disease have been subjected to untold human misery. Because of an archaic belief, they were denied to become a productive member of the society, ostracized and faced social prejudice that exists even today. Hansen's disease is a problem that exists worldwide where numerous legislations (more than 100 legislations across the Globe) discriminate against person experienced with Hansen's disease and deny them basic legitimate rights.

In ancient times, it was considered as divine punishment for heinous crimes, which led to Ostracism & faced Institutionalization, as a result of which a child was separated from his parents, a mother from her children, and so on.

In spite of above only medical aspects of Hansen's disease are being considered and people forgot the social aspects, namely, social, religious & legal discrimination.

As the oldest human rights issue in the world, it should be recognized as a special category of disability. Only few countries have recognized Hansen's disease as a special grade of disability, and have recommended positive affirmations for upliftment of person experienced with Hansen's disease.

In the collection of poetry, we tried to show a full movie from forceful sterilization, isolation to contemporary time. We hope the words will reach millions of social activists across the globe, creating a biosphere of idle activism in the fields of social justice over the coming decade

About The Author

Social Philanthropist & master of psychology--- this is how my engineering chums referred to me when I was in college. Having grown up in a middle class family in Balimela, a beautiful place under the canopy of nature in Odisha, I received my Bachelor's degree in Mechanical Engineering from VSSUT, Burla in 2008.

It was a dream since childhood to do something regarding underprivileged groups of society.

While studying engineering, I visited the Kirba village to teach the children from the economically weaker sections after college hours. In 2006, I also took an active part in solving the street light problem of the village, maybe that was how I got the title of philanthropist from my college chums.

Since 2011, I have been advocating & involved in issues concerning Hansen's disease, disability rights, rights of person experienced with HIV and weaker section of society.

In 2017, a self-financed non- profit organization was founded to advocate for the rights of person experienced with Hansen's disease, Person experienced with HIV and other weaker section of society.

The World Leprosy Community Rights Face book page was designed & developed in February 2018 to promote the rights of person experienced with Hansen's disease.

We have conducted several awareness programs to educate and make people aware regarding the rights of person experienced with Hansen's disease in schools, colleges and colonies.

Secondly, we conducted a survey in 2018 which aimed to determine the current attitude of people towards Hansen's disease, because in order to resolve the problem first you need to identify the gravity of the problem, and perhaps survey is the best tool to identify the problem.

We have distributed food material, masks, soap, and other essentials to several Hansen's colonies located across India, during Covid time, more than 350 person experienced with Hansen's disease benefited from this program.

We have raised several awareness program regarding how to defeat Covid19 through social media as well as in colonies,

There are many echoes in the world but only few voices are there and it is easy to hear the echo than the voice. Since thousand years, however, the voice of a community has gone unheard. They are still fighting for a dignified life.

Around the world, several milestones have been achieved in regards to religion, race, caste or gender. However, the oldest human rights issue (rights of individual experienced from Hansen's disease) was ignored. As of today, across the Globe person's experienced with Hansen's disease are still fighting for dignity.

Several positive affirmations have been made globally to achieve the desired target of social justice regardless of religion, race, gender or disability.

Although, Hansen's disease has been the oldest human rights issue of the world where the rights of person experienced with Hansen's disease are yet to be resolved where they are still struggling to live a dignified life.

In closing, I would like to thank my wife who stood by me & supported me in each step of my life.

Sunil Kumar Sahoo

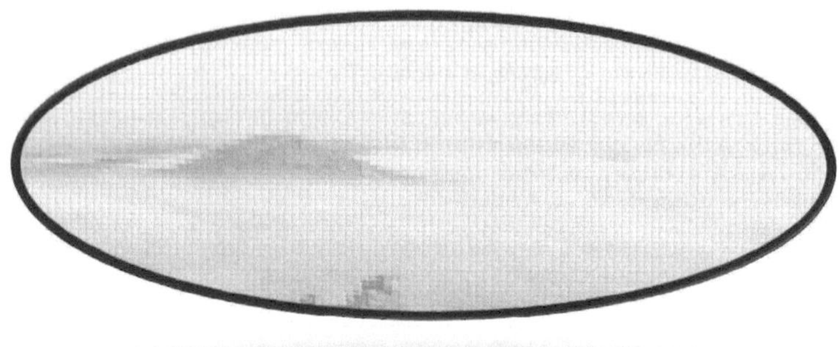

Silence (Shhhhh)

(Silence is the greatest threat to justice. Despite being the oldest human rights issue in the world, the person experienced with Hansen's disease are fighting for their basic legitimate rights like Right to dignity. This poem is to motivate to wake up & to speak out; be vocal about injustice, about the right to equality and a discrimination free biosphere.)

Let's play the game of silence

Where, there is no place for fierceness

Silence regarding my sufferings

Silence regarding my prejudice.

Silence regarding my injustice

Let us play the game of silence

Let us play the game of silence

Compulsory Institutionalization,
Compulsory Segregation,
Compulsory Separation,
Denial for education and
100 discriminatory legislation
Which prevents me from social inclusion
Let us play the game of silence
Let us play the game of silence

Leper's act 1898,
Killed my basic fundamental right
Marriage act 1914,
Slayed me at the age of twenty-Eight
Now, me, my voice, my soul is silence
Let us play the game of silence,
Let us play the game of silence

I was not allowed to cast vote,
I was not allowed for employment,
I was not allowed to travel,
I was not allowed to contest election,

Now, me, my voice,my soul is silence
Let us play the game of silence
Let us play the game of silence

You are silence,
The system is silence,
I am silence,
Let us play the game of silence
Let us play the game of silence

Hundreds of millions died without dignity,
Hundreds are dying without dignity,
Hundreds will die without dignity,
Now, me, my voice, my soul is silence
Let us play the game of silence,
Let us play the game of silence

I am silence, you are silence,
Let us play the game of silence
Let us play the game of silence

I Too Have Right#

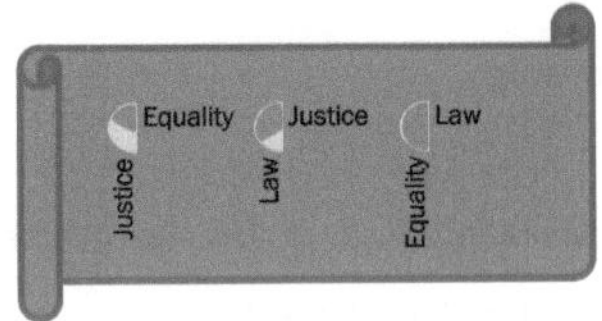

(Around the world, several milestones have been achieved in regards to religion, race, caste or gender. However, the oldest human rights issue (rights of individual experienced from Hansen's disease) was ignored. As of today, across the Globe person's experienced with Hansen's disease are still fighting for dignity.)

I Too Have Rights

Because I am a human being

My voice & my life matters

Because I am a human being

Discrimination, humiliation & untouchability

Now became part of my serendipity

My dream for Love, affection & family

Will never come to reality

100 discriminatory laws

Are against my right to dignity

Denial to education & job

Is against my equal opportunity

Human Rights, civil Rights & Political rights
Now became a matter of fight
4000 years' old disgrace
Became very difficult to countenance

I will become Mandela of our community (When I reborn)
All my dreams will turn into reality
We will create an ideal biosphere,
A domain free of discrimination & delinquency

Oh the lord of justice
Please accept my sacrifice
It's difficult to get justice in this life
Let us hope to get justice in another life (When I reborn)

The Suffering

(The poem shows the untold agony of having Hansen's disease, who had to leave his family behind because he was suffering from it and was forced to live on a lonely island)

The Suffering of my life,

Is very hard to describe

It is the ocean of sorrows

No word can describe

Treated as a demon

Ostracized from the civilization

Abstained my reproductive right

Incarcerated me even when I was right

No instrument can measure my trauma
Since 4000 years I was in coma
I am alive because I am breathing
Since decades my soul found missing

Trauma, depression & suicide
These were three phases of my life
My voice was suppressed on account of law
Each time when I raise my voice,
The society found my flaw
I was separated from my blood relation
Hitting a No Entry Board in my Asylum

The Suffering of my life,
Is very hard to describe
It is the ocean of sorrows
No word can describe

Isolation

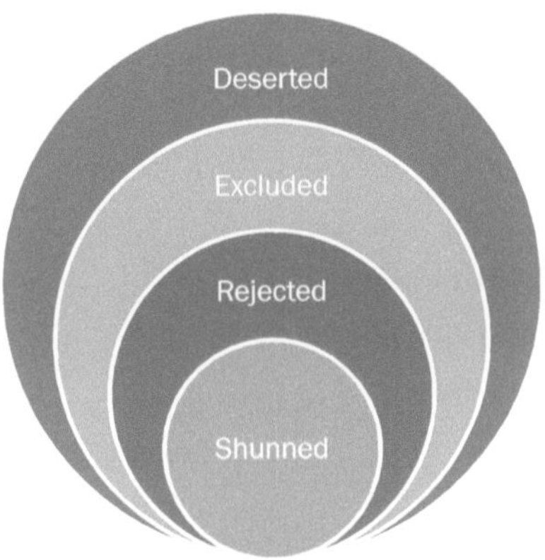

(An excellent poem depicts the tale of sad story of a kid who was taken away from their parents due to Hansen's disease)

Away from society

Away from the habitat

Living in an isle

I am all alone

Ostracized from the colony

Living life of a felony

Separated from family

I am all alone

I am all alone

No siblings, no parent
No caring & no loving
Isolated from society
Exorcized from family
I am all alone
I am all alone

Sorrows have gone
Happiness will come
I am the only king
In my lonely isle

Because I had Leprosy

(This poetry shows social, legal, & religious prejudice against person experienced with Hansen's disease.)

I was abstained from parental property

Because, I had Leprosy

I was denied my social Right

Because I had Leprosy

I was separated from my kids

Because I had leprosy

I was abstained from my last ritual

Because I had leprosy

I was ostracized from society
Because I had leprosy
I was burnt alive in home
Because I had Leprosy

I was not allowed to marry
Because I had Leprosy
I was not allowed to contest election
Because I had Leprosy

Leprosy, Leprosy, Leprosy
It is a disease or a social misery
No one is worried about my right
Join with us in this social fight

I was denied to be treated as kid
Because I had Leprosy
I had faced discrimination in Workplace
Because I had Leprosy

I was not allowed to enter inside religious place
Because I had Leprosy
I was treated as Outcast
Because I had Leprosy

I was denied for a driving license
Because I had Leprosy
I was treated as a Lunatic
Because I had Leprosy

Yet I am fighting for my existence
Leprosy, a disease or a social compulsion
My rights are imperative over other rights
Because I am awakening since million nights (4000 year of injustice)

I Am Leprosy

I am Leprosy

A misunderstood disease

I am Leprosy

The least infectious disease

I am Leprosy

Least dreadful among other disease

Still I am, Discriminated on ground of fallacy

Still I am, Ostracized from friends & Family

I am Leprosy

My suffering is 4000 year's old

An untold story

Which was never told

Before I Die

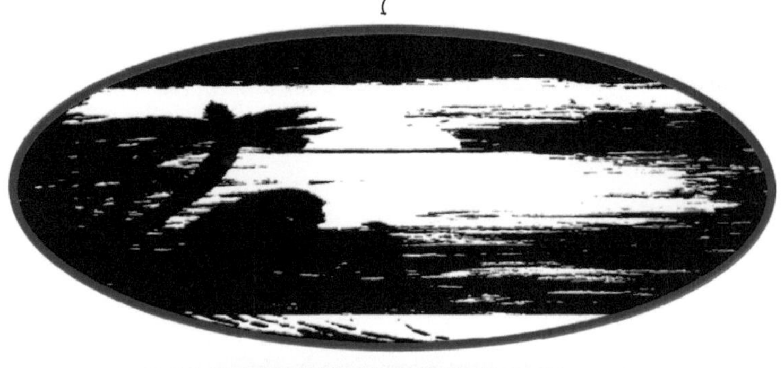

(Imagining a lonely island as a lonely soul taking his last breath causes the poetry to be a picture of suffering)

My last song to you oh my beloved

I do not know whether,

i will be alive or dead by today evening

Oh my beloved,

I will die, i will not breathe

The dawn will arrive and the darkness will cease

Day will come, when poor become richer
The day will arrive today or the sooner
My soul will peep from the heaven
Everything i dreamt is going to happen

Stop exploiting me, It's my democracy
Thanks to the legislation which gives me such legacy

The right of poor will reinstate
Social exploitation will come into cease
Right of our community will be stored
The day will come when,
There will be social fairness &
The dawn will have overwhelmed the darkness

Equality in society
Equality in law
No Discrimination& no social flaw
All that I want to include in our law

Do not treat me as an outcast

Do not treat me as an outcast

Because I had Leprosy

I am just like you as an ordinary man

I am the one as other human

My pen is sharper than the sword

My silence is noisier than a storm

My suffering of life is my power

Revolution for person affected is the need of this hour

I know my words will awake others

People will feel proud for me like others

People of my community will write their story

Discrimination towards leprosy will became history

I believe my words will make a change

The legislation of the globe will acknowledge the change

Justice

Social Justice is my birth right

It should not be a matter of fight

My legislation guarantees

My fundamental & my birth right

Justice, Justice, Justice
We beg social justice,
We beg political justice,
We beg legal justice,
We beg justice, justice, justice

Right to Equality,
Right to Dignity,
Equality in opportunity
And my social right
These are my birth right
It should not be a matter of fight

Let me give equal rights as others
Let me give equal opportunity as others
These are my birth right
It should not be a matter of fight

My Words

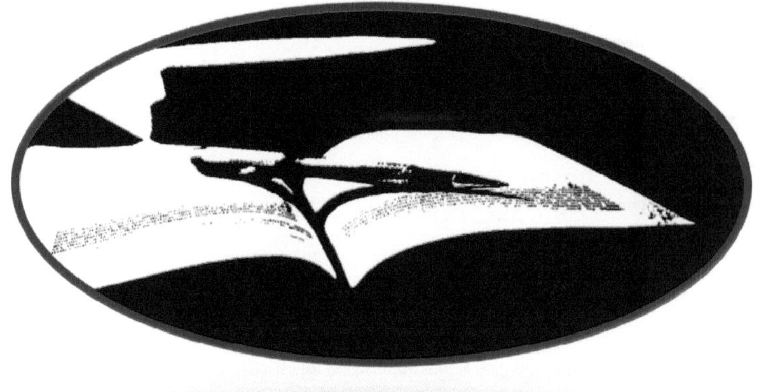

My Words are my power

Which can give filthy a shower

My pen is mightier than the sword

My silence is noisier than the whirlwind

My suffering of life is my power

Revolution is the need of this hour

My people will write their story
Discrimination towards leprosy,
Will be a history

My words are my power
My words are my power
Which gives filthy a shower

Euthansia

Euthanasia, Euthanasia all I need
Because of your hippopotamus deed
You the senators, the law makers
Became converted to social hackers

Humanity, justice & Right to equality,
You forget to include in your glossary
I too deprived of my right
It is all because of your political fight

All I want is a dignified life
Society exorcizes me to an unsocial life
My lesions are bare & blanketed
The year-old wound left me dead
My 4000-year-old wound is difficult to hide
Euthanasia is the only key to die in pride

Social Isolation

Away from society

Away from home

Living in an isle

I am all alone

No brother, no sister

I'm an orphan without Father

Isolated from society

Exorcized from family

I am all alone,
I am all alone

Sorrows have gone
Happiness will come
I am the only king
In my lonely isle

My Unheard Story

My misery, My unheard story
Just Like a text in the slurry
Unheard, Unnoticed blame
That makes me insane
The suffering that never ends
We the people do not have friends

Day by night our pain never ends
No one is here to understand my problem,
& to shake my hands
Like a coffin my sufferings,
Will be buried along with my story
No one here to listen the story of my misery

One day I will die with my poems
Imagine what will be your successors reply to your twins
You the social Hippocrates with crocodile tears
Have to answer the questions with social fears

Discriminated in society,
Discriminated by administration
Discriminated by religion
Discriminated by legislations

Let me die idly in my coffins
Let my feelings to blush like a muffin
My unheard story will make a change
The society & the people will change

I Am All Alone

I am all alone

I am all alone

In this Beautiful world,

In this society,

In the lonely isle

I am all alone

I am all alone

There is no one,
To wipe my tears,
From my eyes
There is no one,
To say a word,
And get rid of my sorrows
I am all alone
I am all alone

You Hippocrates in society
Showing the crocodile tears,
Crocodile tears of equality,
Crocodile tears of social justice,
Now i am dying in a lonely island
Buried alive in a barren land
I am all alone,
I am all alone

Hungry since 50 days
Thirsty since 30 days
Ostracized from society,
Since 80 days
Now i am dying in a lonely island
Buried alive in a barren land
I am all alone
I am all alone

The intellectuals are silent

The senators are silent

The liberals are silent

Everyone is silent

Now i am dying in a lonely island

Buried alive in a barren land

i am all alone

I am all alone

Oh lord, please accomplish my last will,

If i will rebirth,

please do not make me a human being

I do not want to be a Hippocrates

And to show crocodile tears

This is my last will

In the lonely island

Buried alive in a lonely land

i am all alone

I am all alone

Let me enjoy my rights

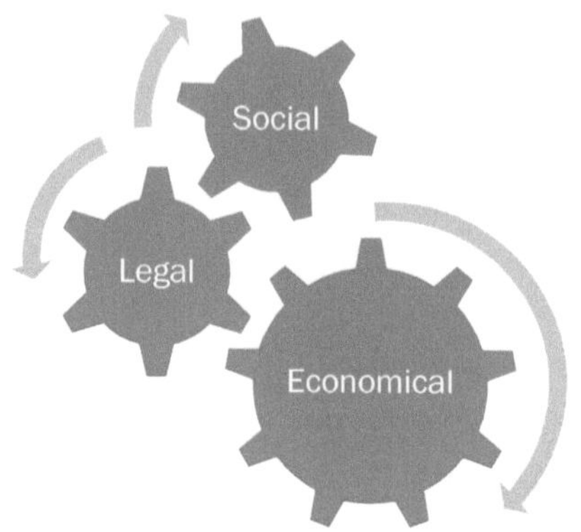

Let me live my life,

Let me utter my words

Let me walk on the road,

Let me cast my vote

Let me feel I am a citizen

Let me enjoy my rights

Let me enjoy my rights

When talking about vote banks,
You talk about legitimate rights.
But When talking about the bonafide matters
You close your shutter & forget our rights.

Suppression, depression & discrimination
Became my destiny ,
I am living life of a felony
Let me enjoy my rights
Let me enjoy my rights

While favoring particular groups,
You forget everything
While looking at real issues
You divert everything

I am fighting for my legitimate rights
Let us join hand in this fight
Let me enjoy my legitimate rights
Let me enjoy my legitimate rights

Illusion

The entire world's a stage
The dream of happiness is a mirage
Living an ostracized life in Molokai
Separated from my beloved,
Who is living in Hawaii

Twinkling Stars in the sky
Are you peeping at my wife?
Golden moon in the sky
Send the message to my wife

Living here is painful
Still here coz I'm afraid to die
A ray of hope to meet you one day
Still here coz I'm afraid to die

I don't know is it true or illusion
Everything seems like a fusion
I heard your voice in the chilliest island
& the noise of your anklet in the bare land

Awake from Sleep

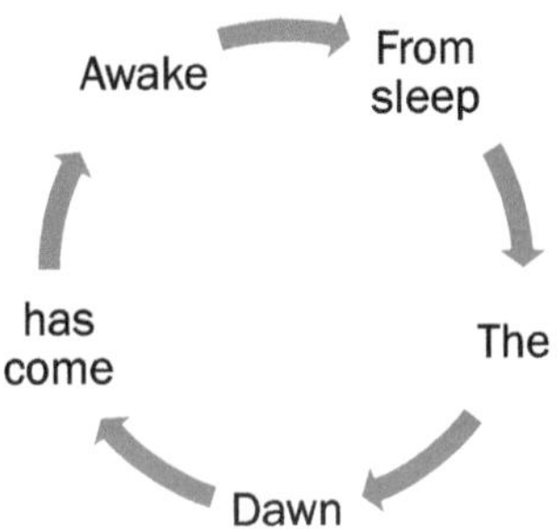

Awake from sleep

The dawn has come

The heavy dusk & the dark night has gone

The dawn of a bright future has come

Awake from sleep, the dawn has come

Awake from sleep, the dawn has come

Ask, the accountability, role& responsibility

To the person who represent the community

Why the 4000 years old problem,

Is still a misery

Who to be hold responsible,

For the misery

Awake from sleep,

The dawn has come

The heavy dusk & the dark night has gone

The heavy dusk & the dark night has gone

Why our voice is so weak

The representative of person affected has to speak

Our inherent right is, Right to equality

Then, why till date we are fighting for dignity

Awake from sleep

The heavy dusk & the dark night has gone

The heavy dusk & the dark night has gone

www.ingramcontent.com/pod-product-compliance
Ingram Content Group UK Ltd.
Pitfield, Milton Keynes, MK11 3LW, UK
UKHW040013200726
13854UKWH00001B/187